Percussion Home Helper
First Lessons at School and at Home

James O. Froseth

with contributions by
Gary W. Hill

GIA Publications, Inc.
Copyright © ℗ 2006
GIA Publications, Inc.
7404 S. Mason Ave.
Chicago, IL 60638
www.giamusic.com
All Rights Reserved.
Produced in the U.S.A.

TABLE OF CONTENTS

GOALS AND OBJECTIVES

Home Helper has two primary goals: 1) to provide your student with the home help needed to develop exemplary performance habits and practice procedures from the start, and 2) to transform early success playing percussion instruments into a lifetime of musical enjoyment and participation.

Objective 1:

To exhibit all the performance skills represented by the players in the photographs.

Step 1:

Look carefully at the photograph to develop a mental image of the physical set-ups you will need to be a successful percussionist.

Objective 2:

To sound as much like the players on the CD as possible.

Step 2:

Listen to bells Track 12 and snare drum Tracks 38, 40, 42, and 44 on your *Home Helper* CD to develop an overall concept of the task you are about to undertake.

KEYS TO SUCCESS

STUDENT – You will be much more likely to succeed if you:

1) take proper care of your instruments,
2) read every word of the text and follow all instructions,
3) practice with the CD every day,
4) follow the lead of your teacher, and
5) attend every lesson at school equipped to play and prepared to learn.

HOME HELPER – You will be most helpful to your student if you:

1) help your student to take proper care of their instruments,
2) read every word of the text,
3) monitor practice sessions regularly,
4) encourage your student to practice with the CD every day,
5) check off each achievement on every CHECKLIST once each week (remember, every check is a motivating "pat on the back"),
6) avoid negative comments,
7) give your student lots of attention, and
8) communicate with the teacher through your *Home Helper* book when questions or concerns arise.

TEACHER – You will be most helpful to your student if you:

1) recognize and record student achievement, and
2) coordinate the home helper's efforts with school instruction.

GUIDELINES FOR PRODUCTIVE PRACTICE ON THE BELLS

Guiding principle: Practice must have purpose.

Step 1: Decide what it is you want to accomplish. For example:

1. **"I want to improve my:"**
   A. Playing Position (page 4)
   B. Left Hand Grip (page 4)
   C. Right Hand Grip (page 4)
   D. Left Hand Stroke (page 5)
   E. Right Hand Stroke (page 6)
   F. Alternating Stroke (page 7)

2. **"I want to improve my ability to listen and play what I hear."** (Tracks 2, 3, and 4, on page 5, Tracks 5, 6, and 7 on page 6, Tracks 8, 9, and 10 on page 7, and Track 11 on page 8)

3. **"I want to sound more like the player on the CD when I play** *Practice Every Day March*.**"** (Track 12 on page 8)

GUIDELINES FOR PRODUCTIVE PRACTICE ON THE SNARE DRUM

Guiding principle: Practice must have purpose.

Step 1: Decide what it is you want to accomplish. For example:

1. **"I want to improve my":**
   A. Playing Position (page 11)
   B. Right Hand Grip (page 12)
   C. Right Hand Stroke (page 12)
   D. Left Hand Grip (page 13)
   E. Left Hand Stroke (page 13)
   F. Alternating Stroke (page 14)

2. **"I want to improve my ability to listen and play what I hear."** (Tracks 14, 15, and 16 on page 12, Tracks 17, 18, and 19 on page 13, Tracks 20, 21, and 22 on page 14, Tracks 24–30 on page 15, Tracks 31–37 on page 16)

3. **"I want to sound more like the player on the CD when I play the snare drum accompaniment to** *Practice Every Day March*.**"** (Tracks 38, 40, 42, and 44 on page 16)

RECOMMENDATIONS

1. Schedule several short practice sessions daily rather than one extended session.

2. Take frequent breaks during practice sessions to avoid fatigue.

3. Be spontaneous. Practice whenever you feel motivated to make music or improve your performance skills.

4. Encourage your adult home helper to oversee your practice as often as possible.

5. Schedule a regular weekly session for your adult home helper to enter achievement marks on every CHECKLIST.

BELLS PLAYING POSITION

Step 1: Position the bells slightly below your waist and to the center of your body.

Step 2: Position your arms and elbows comfortably to the side of your body.

Step 3: Stand in a position that places the heads of the mallets over the center of the first row of tone bars.

Note: You should feel well balanced and free of tension.

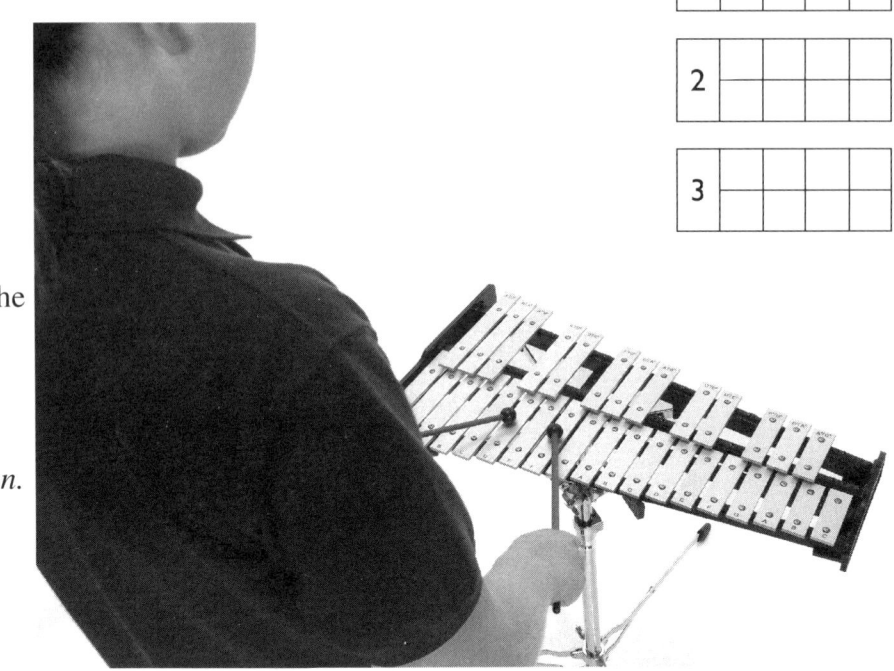

	MARK ✔ or ? HERE			
Step	Week			
	1	2	3	4
	5	6	7	8
1				
2				
3				

KEYBOARD MALLET GRIP

Step 1: Grip each mallet between your thumb and the first joint of your first finger.

Step 2: Wrap your fingers around each mallet without touching the mallet shaft.

Note: Keep your wrists straight and relaxed.

	MARK ✔ or ? HERE			
Step	Week			
	1	2	3	4
	5	6	7	8
1				
2				

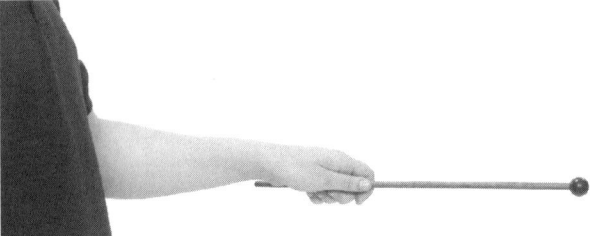

Left Hand

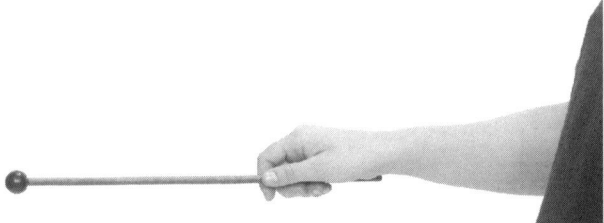

Right Hand

KEYBOARD MALLET STROKE - LEFT HAND

Step 1: Position the left hand mallet in the "ready position" 2 to 3 inches over the keyboard.

Step 2: Raise the mallet 3 inches, drop it to the tone bar and bring it back to the "ready position" as quickly as possible.

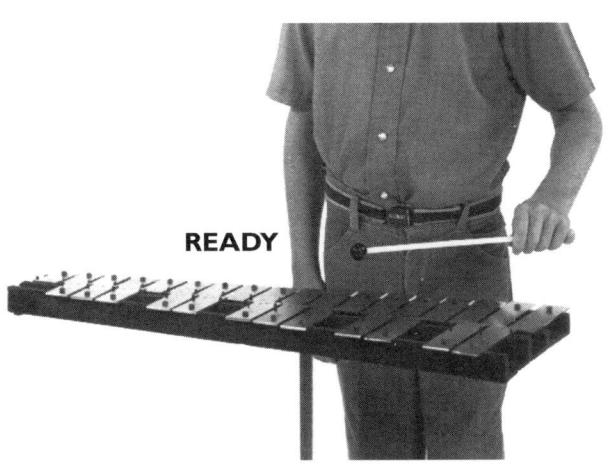

READY

Note: The best tones are produced when the mallet head is in contact with the tone bar for as short a time as possible.

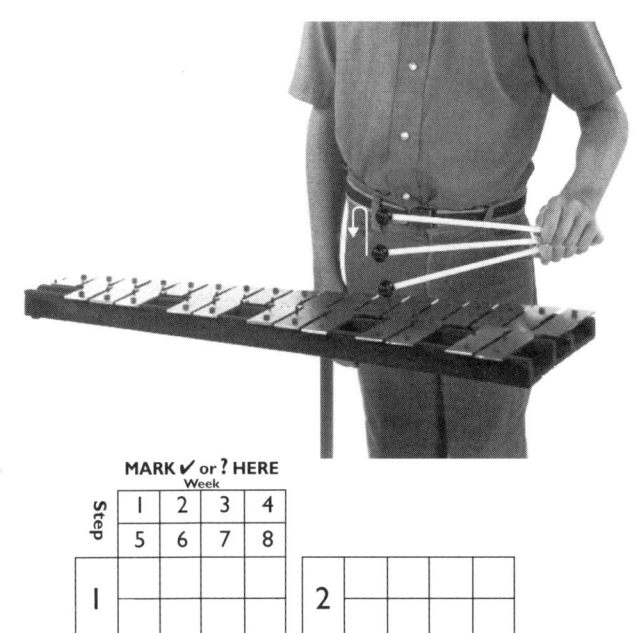

MARK ✔ or ? HERE

Step	Week 1	2	3	4
	5	6	7	8

1						2				

PRODUCING THE TONE "D" ON THE BELLS

FIRST TONE: "D"

D

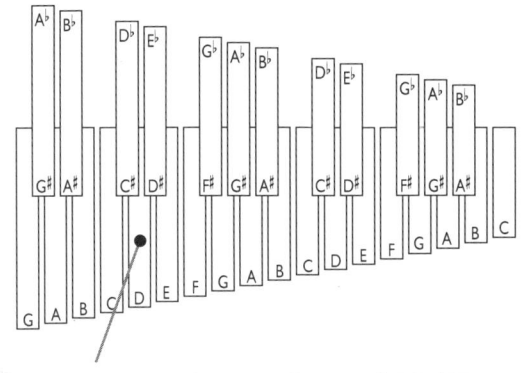

CD Track 2 *LISTEN TO THE CD and PLAY*

CD Track 3 *LISTEN TO THE CD and PLAY*

CD Track 4 *Call and Response – First Tone "D"*

A. The left hand mallet grip is acceptable.

B. The left hand mallet stroke is acceptable.

C. The tone quality resembles the model.

MARK ✔ or ? HERE

Step	Week 1	2	3	4
	5	6	7	8

A				

B				

C				

KEYBOARD MALLET STROKE - RIGHT HAND

Step 1: Position the right hand mallet in the "ready position" 2 to 3 inches over the keyboard.

Step 2: Raise the mallet 3 inches, drop it to the tone bar, and bring it back to the "ready position" as quickly as possible.

Step	MARK ✔ or ? HERE Week			
	1	2	3	4
	5	6	7	8
1				
2				

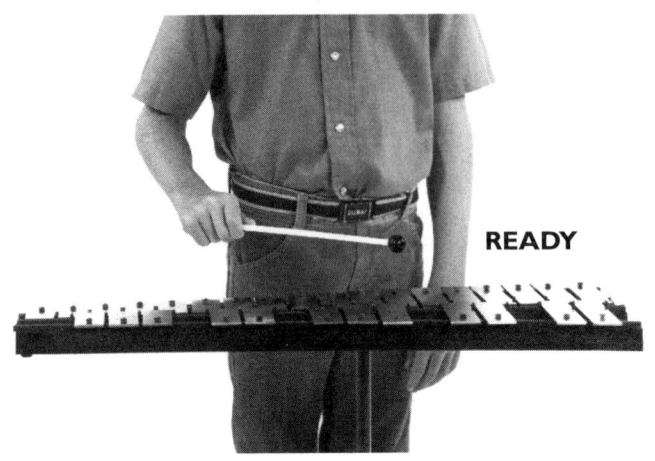

READY

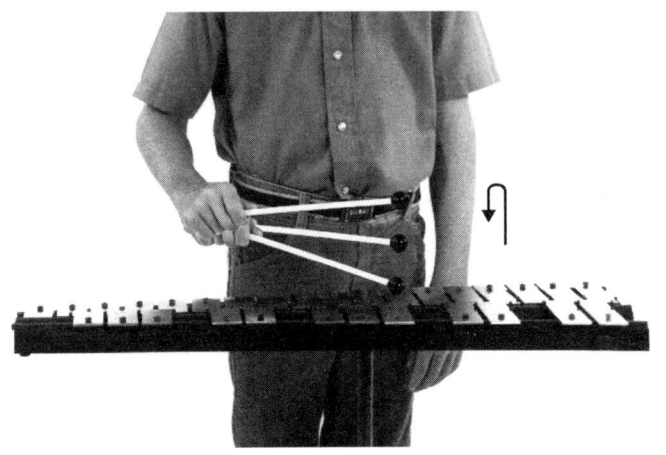

PRODUCING THE TONE "E♭" ON THE BELLS

SECOND TONE: "E♭"

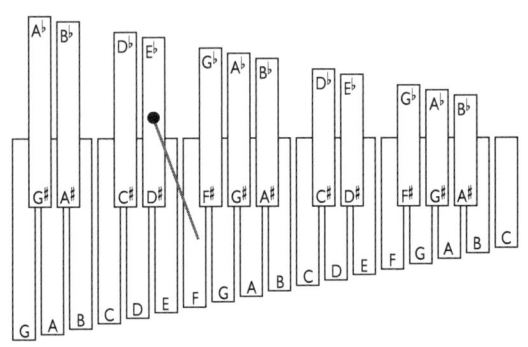

CD Track 5 *LISTEN TO THE CD and PLAY*   **CD Track 6** *LISTEN TO THE CD and PLAY*

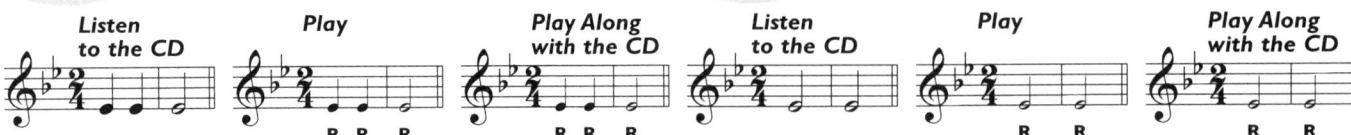

CD Track 7 *Call and Response – First Tone "D" and Second Tone "E♭"*

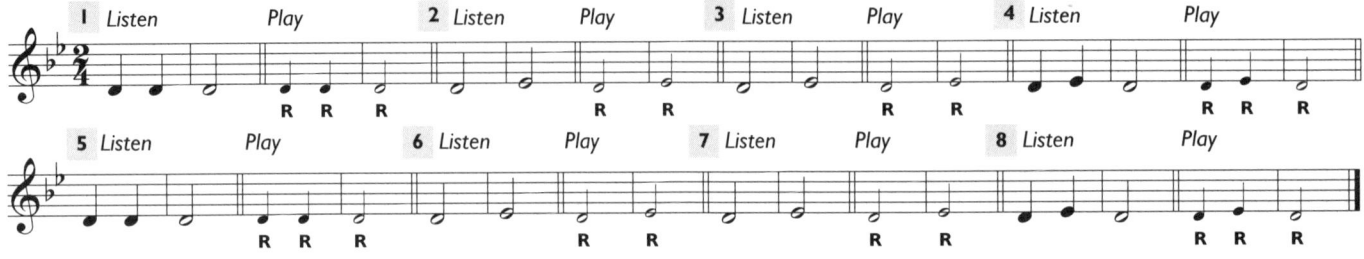

A. The right hand mallet grip is acceptable.
B. The right hand mallet stroke is acceptable.
C. The tone quality resembles the model.

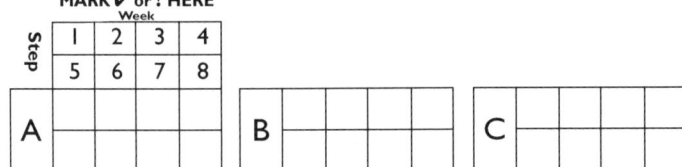

Step	MARK ✔ or ? HERE Week			
	1	2	3	4
	5	6	7	8
A				
B				
C				

THE ALTERNATING KEYBOARD MALLET STROKE

Step 1: Position both mallets in the "ready position" 3 inches over the keyboard.

Step 2: Raise the left mallet 3 inches, drop it to the tone bar, and bring it back to the "ready position" as quickly as possible.

Step 3: Raise the right mallet 3 inches, drop it to the tone bar, and bring it back to the "ready position" as quickly as possible.

MARK ✔ or ? HERE

Step	Week			
	1	2	3	4
	5	6	7	8
1				

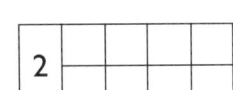

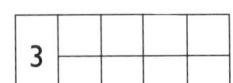

PRODUCING THE TONE "F" ON THE BELLS

THIRD TONE: "F"

F

CD Track 8 *LISTEN TO THE CD and PLAY*

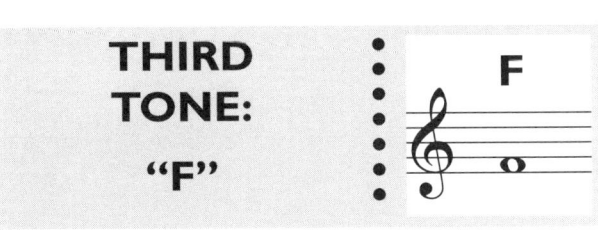

CD Track 9 *LISTEN TO THE CD and PLAY*

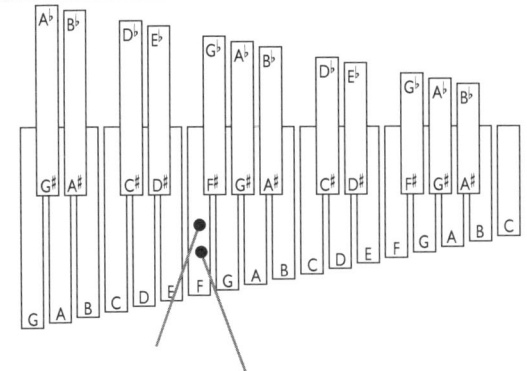

CD Track 10 *Call and Response – First Tone "D," Second Tone "E♭," and Third Tone "F"*

A. The right hand mallet grip and stroke are acceptable.
B. The left hand mallet grip and stroke are acceptable.
C. The tone quality resembles the model.

MARK ✔ or ? HERE

Step	Week			
	1	2	3	4
	5	6	7	8
A				

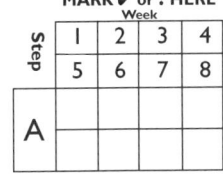

FIRST TUNE

Preparation to Play *Practice Every Day March*

CD Track 11 *Listen and Play*

March Tempo

Practice Every Day March - Bells

CD Track 12 **1.** *Listen* **2.** *Listen and Play Along*   **CD Track 13** *Play*

Prac - tice ev' - ry day; If you do you'll learn to play!

A. Tone quality and pitch resemble the recorded model.

B. The performance is rhythmically synchronized with the accompaniment.

		MARK ✔ or ? HERE Week			
Step		1	2	3	4
		5	6	7	8
A					
B					

STICKING PRINCIPLES FOR KEYBOARD INSTRUMENTS

PRINCIPLE 1
Play large descending intervals right hand to left hand (R-L). See Example 1.

PRINCIPLE 2
Play large ascending intervals left hand to right hand (L-R). See Example 2.

PRINCIPLE 3
When there are two or more large descending intervals, stick right hand to left hand on the largest interval. See Example 3.

PRINCIPLE 4
When there are two or more large ascending intervals, stick left hand to right hand on the largest interval. See Example 4.

PRINCIPLE 5
When a large ascending interval and a large descending interval are separated by a repeated note or a smaller ascending or descending interval, set-up the large intervals when possible by double sticking the repeated note or smaller interval. See Examples 5 and 6.

PRINCIPLE 6
There are many ways to solve a given sticking problem. Experiment, improvise, and develop the ability to solve sticking problems independently and in a manner that is easiest and most comfortable for you.

PARTS OF THE CONCERT SNARE DRUM

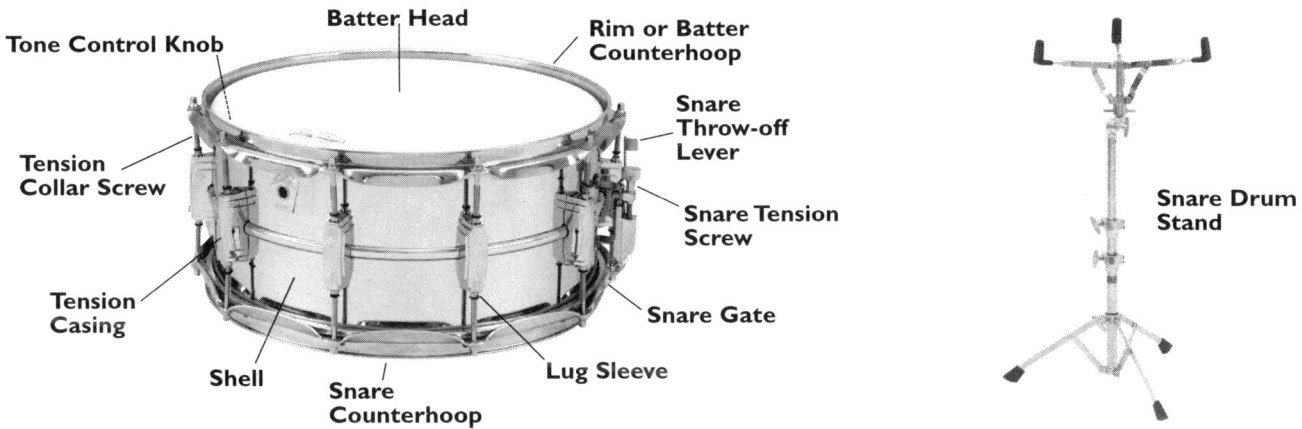

Tone Control Knob
Batter Head
Rim or Batter Counterhoop
Snare Throw-off Lever
Tension Collar Screw
Snare Tension Screw
Tension Casing
Snare Gate
Shell
Snare Counterhoop
Lug Sleeve
Snare Drum Stand

CARE OF THE SNARE DRUM

Your snare drum is a fragile instrument that requires special care. Satisfactory progress is possible only if your instrument is in proper playing condition. If anything should go wrong with your drum (or your bells), DO NOT ATTEMPT YOUR OWN REPAIRS. Only a qualified repair person has the experience and skill to service your instruments. If you need advice, consult your teacher or your music dealer.

Proper instrument care begins with clean hands. Always wash your hands before playing your instrument. Clean hands will help to keep your drum clean and technically sound. Wipe the metal shell and tension casings with a soft, clean cloth after each playing. Occasionally, use a high grade metal polish to clean the shell and tension casings. Approximately once every six months, lightly lubricate all tension rod threads at the point where they enter the tension casings. Also, place a drop of light oil on the threads of the snare strainer screw.

A well-tuned snare drum that is clean and properly lubricated does not require daily or even weekly adjustment. Adjust your snare drum only when it is absolutely necessary. Learn the parts of your drum, and check frequently for loose or missing parts.

Keep your instrument in its case when you are not playing it to avoid damage and costly repairs. Always secure the latches immediately after you close the case. Do not force books, music, CD cases, or other items into the case on top of the instrument or beside it. Avoid exposing your snare drum to extreme heat or cold, moisture or excessive humidity, sharp blows, dust or dirt, or other possible sources of damage.

THE SNARE DRUM STICK

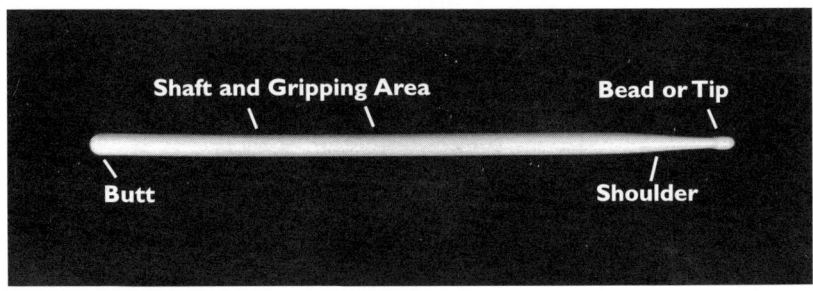

Shaft and Gripping Area
Bead or Tip
Butt
Shoulder

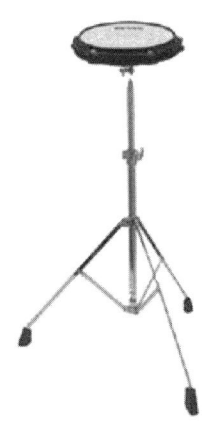

USING A PRACTICE PAD

The practice pad is a very useful device. It allows the percussionist to practice quietly virtually anywhere and at any time. The practice pad should be mounted on a stand to insure the correct playing angle and height.

Practice Pad on a Stand

THE CONCERT SNARE DRUM SET-UP

Step 1: Position the stand in front of you so that the single holding arm is to your left.

Step	Week			
	1	2	3	4
	5	6	7	8
1				

Step 2: Raise the stand to a position that will place it 14 inches to 16 inches below your waist and tighten the height adjustment screw.

Step 3: Pull the single arm out to its full length, and spread the double holding arms.

Step 4: Level the holding arms, and tighten the angle adjustment screw.

2				

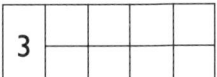

3				

4				

Step 5: Lower the drum at a downward angle onto the double holding arms and then down onto the single holding arm.

Note: The snare throw-off assembly must face you.

Step 6: Slide the single holding arm in to secure the drum.

Step 7: Adjust the height of the stand, if necessary, to position the drum 6 to 8 inches below your waist.

5				

6				

7				

SNARE DRUM PLAYING POSITION

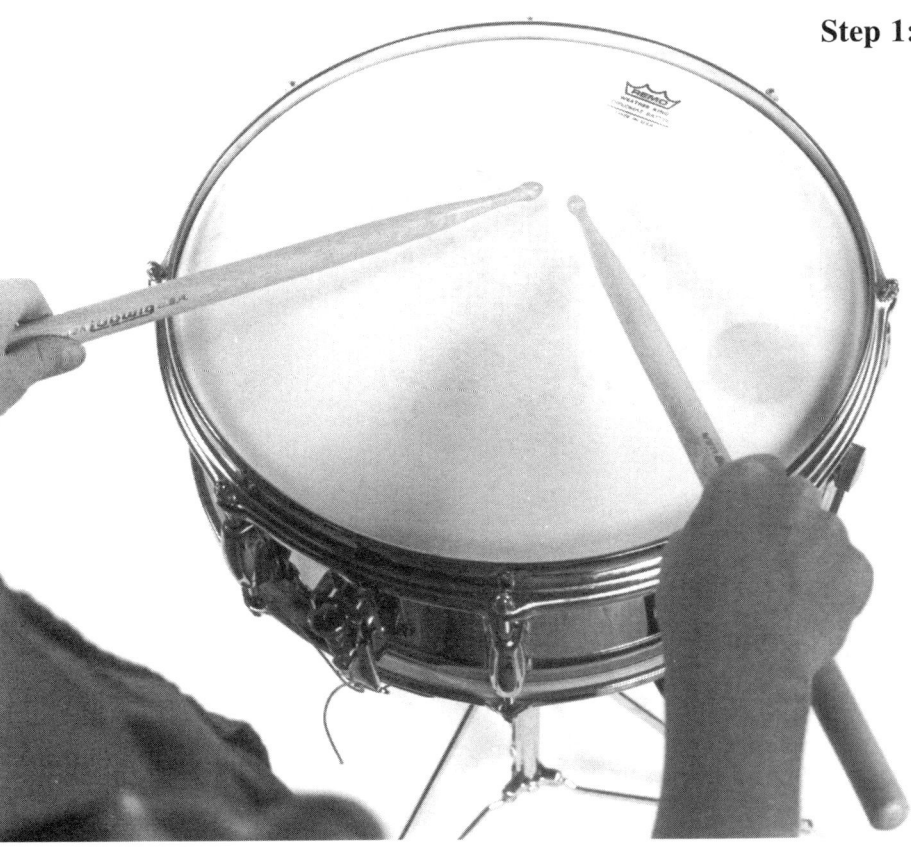

Step 1: Stand to the drum at a position that places the tips of the sticks slightly off the center of the head.

Step 2: Position the snare drum 6 to 8 inches below your waist.

Step 3: Position your elbows comfortably away from your body.

Note: You should feel well balanced and free of tension.

	MARK ✔ or ? HERE		
	Week		
Step	1	2	3	4
	5	6	7	8
1				
2				
3				

THE MATCHED GRIP - RIGHT HAND

Step 1: Grip the stick between your thumb and the first joint of your first finger about one-third of the way up from the end of the stick.

Step 2: Curve your fingers around the stick.

Step 3: Position your hand palm down with the stick approximately parallel to the ground.

Note: If the grip is correct, the drumstick will feel balanced and it will pivot freely between your thumb and first finger.

	MARK ✔ or ? HERE

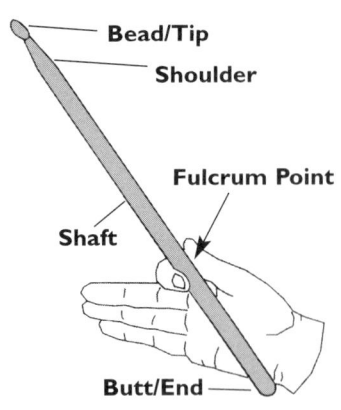

Bead/Tip
Shoulder
Fulcrum Point
Shaft
Butt/End

Step	Week			
	1	2	3	4
	5	6	7	8
1				
2				
3				

THE RIGHT HAND SNARE DRUM STROKE

Step 1: Position the right hand drumstick in the "ready position" 2 to 3 inches over the drum head.

Step 2: Raise the drumstick 3 inches, drop it to the drum head, and bring it back to the "ready position" as quickly as possible.

READY

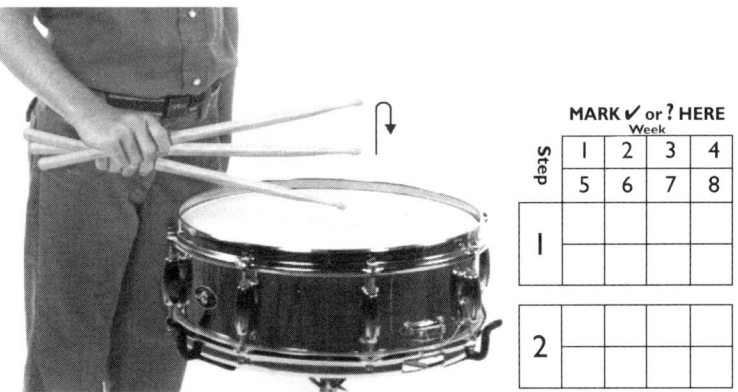

MARK ✔ or ? HERE				
Step	Week			
	1	2	3	4
	5	6	7	8
1				
2				

CD Track 14 *LISTEN TO THE CD and PLAY*   **CD Track 15** *LISTEN TO THE CD and PLAY*

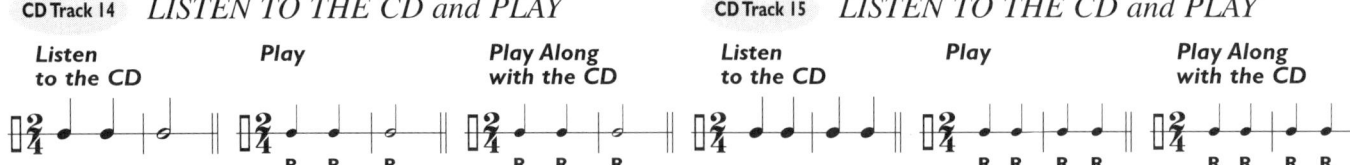

CD Track 16 *Call and Response – Listen and Play*

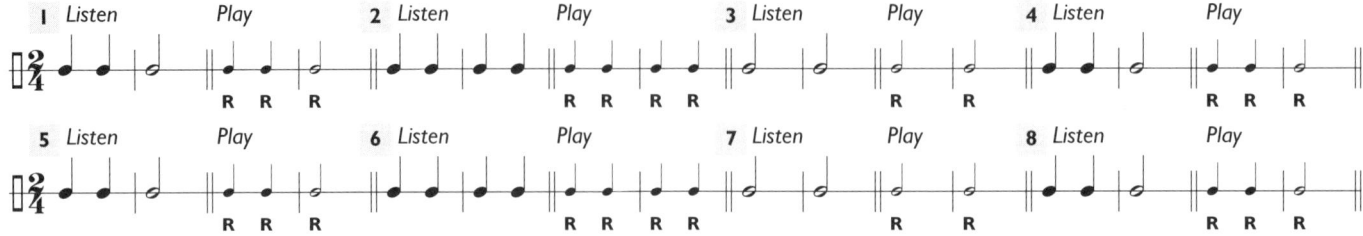

A. The right hand grip and stroke are acceptable.

B. The tone quality resembles the model.

C. The rhythmic patterns match the model.

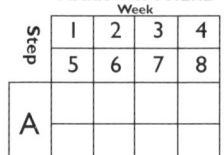

MARK ✔ or ? HERE				
Step	Week			
	1	2	3	4
	5	6	7	8

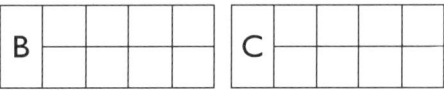

A | | | | |
B | | | | |
C | | | | |

THE MATCHED GRIP - LEFT HAND

Step 1: Grip the stick between your thumb and the first joint of your first finger about one-third of the way up from the end of the stick.

Step 2: Curve your fingers around the stick.

Step 3: Position your hand palm down with the stick approximately parallel to the ground.

Note: If the grip is correct, the drumstick will feel balanced, and it will pivot freely between your thumb and first finger.

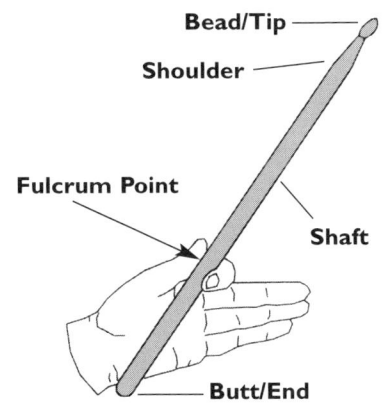

		Week			
	Step	1	2	3	4
		5	6	7	8
1					
2					
3					

MARK ✔ or ? HERE

THE LEFT HAND SNARE DRUM STROKE

Step 1: Position the left hand drumstick in the "ready position" 2 to 3 inches over the drum head.

Step 2: Raise the drumstick 3 inches, drop it to the drum head, and bring it back to the "ready position" as quickly as possible.

READY

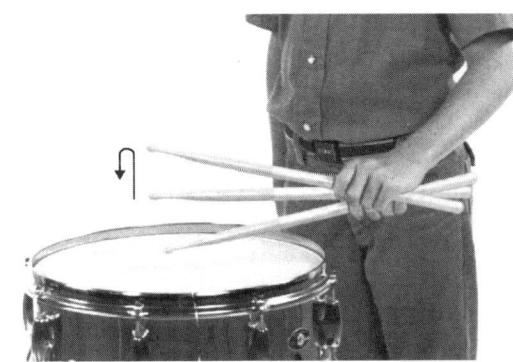

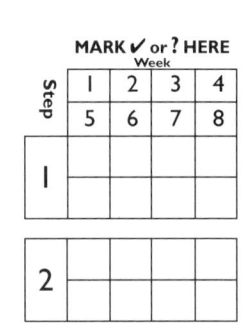

MARK ✔ or ? HERE

CD Track 17 *LISTEN TO THE CD and PLAY*   **CD Track 18** *LISTEN TO THE CD and PLAY*

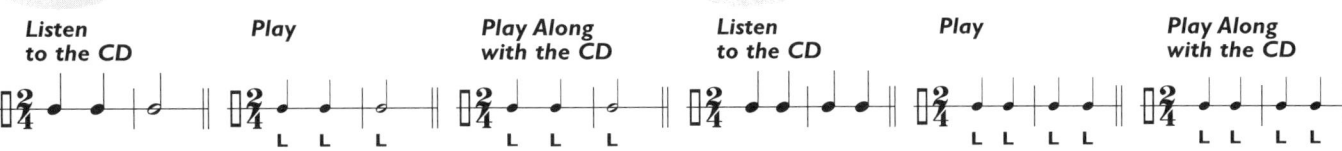

CD Track 19 *Call and Response – Listen and Play*

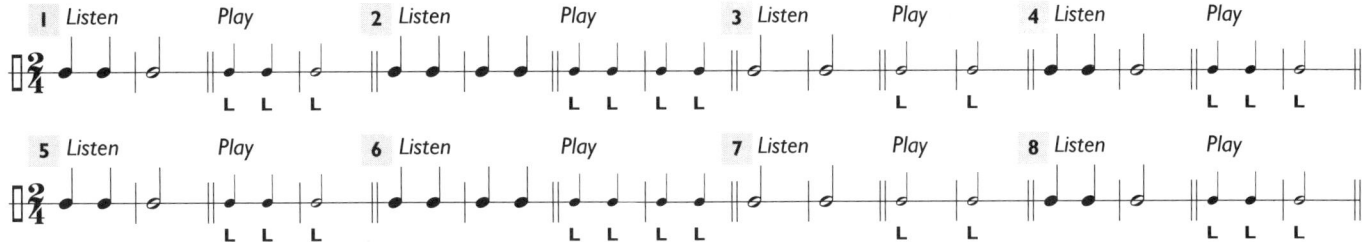

A. The left hand grip and stroke are acceptable.
B. The tone quality resembles the model.
C. The rhythmic patterns match the model.

THE ALTERNATING SNARE DRUM STROKE

Step 1: Position both drumsticks in the "ready position" 2 to 3 inches over the drum head.

Step 2: Raise the right hand drumstick 3 inches, drop it to the drum head, and bring it back to the "ready position" as quickly as possible.

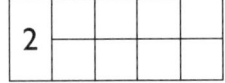

Step 3: Raise the left hand drumstick 3 inches, drop it to the drum head, and bring it back to the "ready position" as quickly as possible.

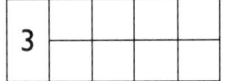

CD Track 20 *LISTEN TO THE CD and PLAY*   **CD Track 21** *LISTEN TO THE CD and PLAY*

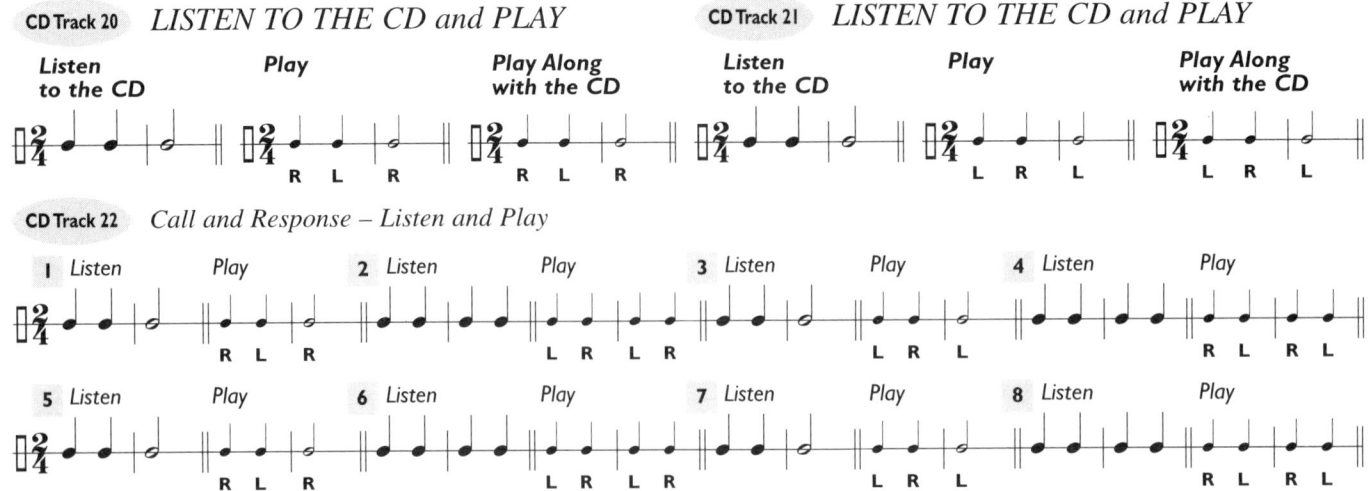

A. The left hand grip and stroke are acceptable.
B. The right hand grip and stroke are acceptable.
C. The tone quality resembles the model.
D. The rhythmic patterns match the model.

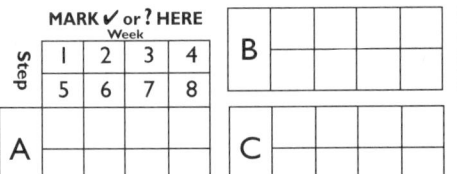

THE MULTIPLE BOUNCE (BUZZ) ROLL

Step 1: Position the right hand drumstick over the batter head in the "ready position."

Step 2: Raise the drumstick 3 inches, drop it to the head, and let it bounce freely until it comes to rest on the head.

Note: If the hand position is correct and the fingers are placed around the stick in a relaxed manner, the result will be a "buzz" sound.

	MARK ✔ or ? HERE Week			
Step	1	2	3	4
	5	6	7	8
1				
2				

CD Track 23 *THE MULTIPLE BOUNCE (BUZZ) ROLL - JUST LISTEN*

The Right Hand Multiple Bounce (Closed) Roll

CD Track 24 *LISTEN TO THE CD and PLAY*   **CD Track 25** *LISTEN TO THE CD and PLAY*

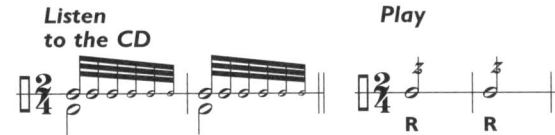 

The Left Hand Multiple Bounce (Closed) Roll

CD Track 26 *LISTEN TO THE CD and PLAY*   **CD Track 27** *LISTEN TO THE CD and PLAY*

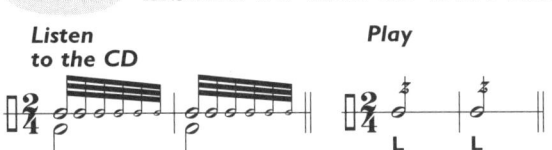 

The Alternating Multiple Bounce (Closed) Roll

CD Track 28 *LISTEN TO THE CD and PLAY*   **CD Track 29** *LISTEN TO THE CD and PLAY*

CD Track 30 *Call and Response – Listen and Play*

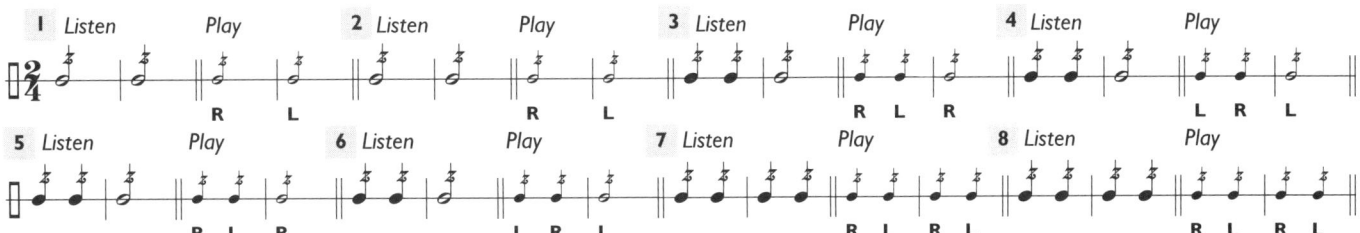

A. The left hand grip and multiple bounce stroke are acceptable.
B. The right hand grip and multiple bounce stroke are acceptable.
C. The tone quality resembles the model.
D. The sticking patterns are correct.

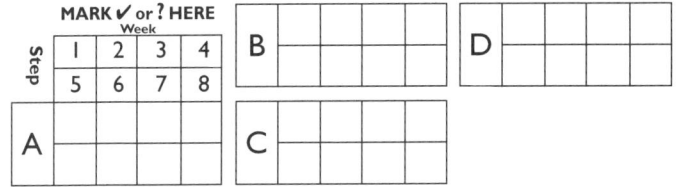

THE SNARE DRUM MUSICAL PLAY ALONG

PREPARATION FOR SNARE DRUM "PLAY ALONG"

CD Track 31 *LISTEN TO THE CD and PLAY*

Listen to the CD — Play — Play Along with the CD
RLRL R / RLRL R

CD Track 32 *LISTEN TO THE CD and PLAY*

Listen to the CD — Play — Play Along with the CD
LRLR L / LRLR L

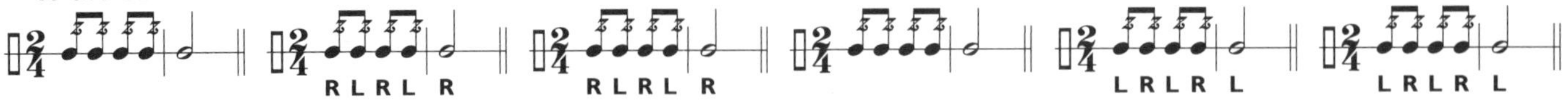

CD Track 33 *LISTEN TO THE CD and PLAY*

Listen to the CD — Play — Play Along with the CD
RLR LRL / RLR LRL

CD Track 34 *LISTEN TO THE CD and PLAY*

Listen to the CD — Play — Play Along with the CD
LRL RLR / LRL RLR

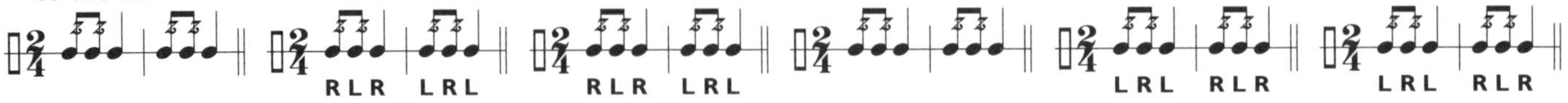

CD Track 35 *LISTEN TO THE CD and PLAY*

Listen to the CD — Play — Play Along with the CD
RLRL RLR / RLRL RLR

CD Track 36 *LISTEN TO THE CD and PLAY*

Listen to the CD — Play — Play Along with the CD
LRLR LRL / LRLR LRL

CD Track 37 *Preparation to Play* Practice Every Day March *Accompaniments*

1 Listen — Play: R L R
2 Listen — Play: L R
3 Listen — Play: L R L R
4 Listen — Play: L R L

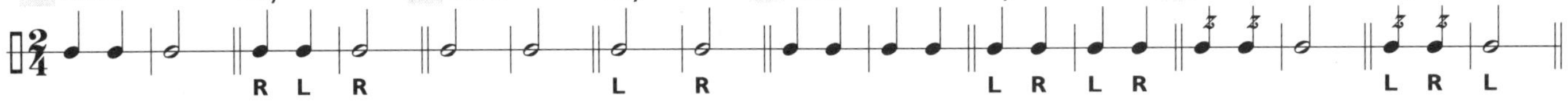

5 Listen — Play: R L R L
6 Listen — Play: RLR LRL
7 Listen — Play: RLRL R
8 Listen — Play: LRLR LRL

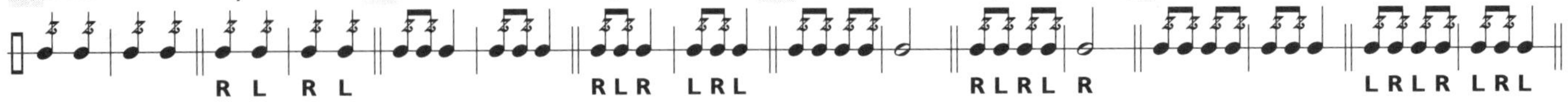

9 Listen — Play: R L R L
10 Listen — Play: RLR LRL
11 Listen — Play: RLRL R
12 Listen — Play: LRLR LRL

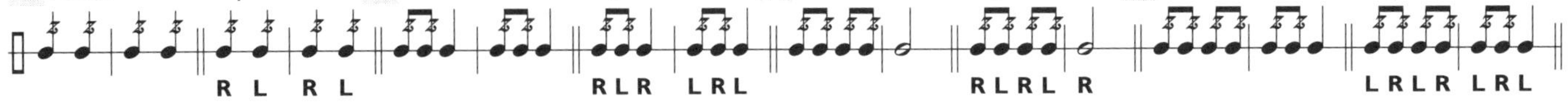

SNARE DRUM ACCOMPANIMENTS FOR *PRACTICE EVERY DAY MARCH* "PLAY ALONG"

Accompaniment 1

CD Track 38 Model — **CD Track 39** Play Along

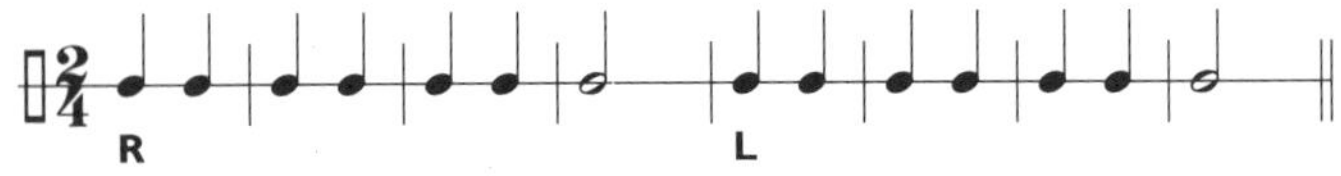

R — L

Accompaniment 2

CD Track 40 Model — **CD Track 41** Play Along

R — L

Accompaniment 3

CD Track 42 Model — **CD Track 43** Play Along

R — L

Accompaniment 4

CD Track 44 Model — **CD Track 45** Play Along

R — L

THE MULTIPLE BOUNCE (BUZZ) ROLL - SLOW TO FAST

CD Track 46 **CD Track 47**

Model — Play Along

A. The left hand grip and stroke are acceptable.
B. The right hand grip and stroke are acceptable.
C. The tone quality resembles the model.
D. The sticking patterns are correct.

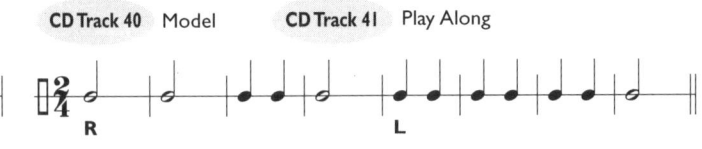

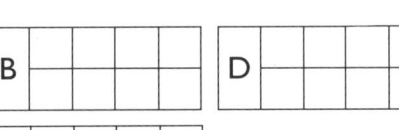
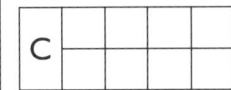

MARK ✔ or ? HERE

Step	Week 1	2	3	4
	5	6	7	8

A | | | |

B | | | |

C | | | |

D | | | |